Magic in the Bible

Ken Goudsward

ISBN: 978-1-9992160-8-5

Dimensionfold.com

Contents

Foreword

There is a fine line between miracles and magic. On the one hand, Sarah Bessey, a British Columbia author and speaker, once wrote a book entitled *Miracles and Other Reasonable Things*. On the other, Arthur C. Clark, the British writer of ground-breaking science fiction, many years ago reminded us that any sufficiently advanced technology is indistinguishable from magic. Harry Potter and Gandalf live in the hearts of people everywhere. But many contemporary Evangelical pastors warn their flocks to stay away from such fictional characters, even though the world of Gandalf and his band of wizards came from the fertile imagination of a staunch Christian churchman. The book *Real Magic: Ancient Wisdom, Modern Science, and a Guide to the Secret Power of the Universe*, has become a world-wide best seller, reprinted in several languages. Dean Radin, PhD, the author, is a sober-minded and meticulous scientist who conducts research at the Institute for Noetic Sciences, but many of his colleagues refuse to take his work seriously.

Clearly, miracles are popular these days. But magic is even more so. Is there really much of a difference?

Ken Goudsward rightly points out that much of the miracle vs. magic debate within Christianity is as much about contemporary definitions as theological substance. In most circles, miracles are seen as coming from God. Magic, at least in much of popular culture, has somehow become cloaked in dark layers of divination and sorcery. Even most stage magicians prefer the word "illusionist" to describe what they are doing, the better to avoid being painted over with cultural images of mysterious activities carried out at the dark of the moon by masked and diabolic practitioners.

It is a sad but unavoidable truth that too often cultural prejudices override religious interpretations. It is easy and much too common to *first* believe something, and *then* seek textual justification for that which has already been decided. Is that what has happened in modern religious sects who teach their adherents to avoid any study of magic? Miracles, they say, are recognized as bonafide because they are performed by God. Magic is carried out by human agents, at best, and demon-inspired counterfeits at worst. It is thus forbidden in many Christian circles.

What is the poor believer to do, however, when he or she comes across real magic, performed by real people, in the Bible? What, for instance, are they to make of the words of Jesus in John 14? When confronted with the fact that he has done things that look suspiciously like magic, he says very plainly, "Whoever believes in me will do the works I have been doing, and they will do even greater things than these." It seems as though a straight-forward reading reveals that not only was Jesus performing magic, he expected his followers to do so as well.

Why are walking on water and calming a storm considered to be a miracle rather than a magic trick? Both are done by transforming the laws of physics. Both are the stock in trade of many modern illusionists.

That opens up a veritable Pandora's Box of questions — questions that demand to be fully addressed lest they hide in the dark recesses of our minds, peeking out at awkward moments of doubt throughout our lives.

This is exactly what Ken Goudsward attempts to do in the book you are now about to engage. He opens up the Bible and fearlessly examines the evidence. There is no other way to confront the issue. What is magic? What are miracles? Is one bad and one good? Is one to be allowed and one forbidden? That is the subject before us.

Before you begin to read, however, I need to share a story with you that confronts the whole issue of miracles and magic and reveals that the two often can have similar meanings and applications.

I once a had a good friend who was a doctor serving in a big-city hospital. He told me a story that transpired early in his residency about testing a new drug that had not been fully approved for commercial use. It had made its way slowly up through the careful protocols needed for such a process, and was about to be administered to a group of patients who had been approved for the study. They were all given a bright red capsule and told it was an experimental drug that would cure their illness. What they didn't know was that half of them were taking a sugar pill.

As expected, the group who had received the real medicine experienced a statistically important result. Many more than half of them were cured. The experiment was pronounced a success and the pill has now been successfully prescribed for many years. It's a standard weapon in the typical arsenal of medications used regularly today.

But what was interesting to me was something my friend confided that had him stumped. A statistically meaningful proportion of the group that had been issued sugar pills got better, too. As a student, my friend was fascinated. How had those who had received no real medicine at all managed to find healing?

He asked his mentor, the doctor who had managed the experiment.

"It's called the placebo effect," he was told. "Sometimes a sugar pill works like magic."

"Why?" my friend wondered.

The reply he received was this: "No one knows. It's a miracle."

Magic or miracle? Perhaps, in the end, there is no difference. You be the judge.

- Jim Willis

Jim Willis is the author of over a dozen books including *Supernatural Gods: Spiritual Mysteries, Psychic Experiences, and Scientific Truths* and *The Religion Book: Places, Prophets, Saints, and Seers*

Introduction

Magic has had a tumultuous relationship to Christianity through the ages. The Spanish inquisition and the Salem witch trials of 17th century America are prime examples of what can go terribly wrong when well-intentioned people take it upon themselves to act on their best understanding of scripture, and enforce their beliefs onto others who may or may not agree. What if those perpetrators were wrong? Oh, well I mean, of course they were wrong, weren't they. I mean, we are much more enlightened today aren't we? Christians may not go around burning people at the stake, at least not physically, but is that just because they have better impulse control? Or perhaps because of a more defined justice system that won't overlook such piety-fueled fervor? Are our boundaries simply better defined? Is it possible that some of the same underlying assumptions that drove the witch hunters remain lying nascent in modern religion?

A pervasive taboo permeates modern Christianity. It is an ancient and entrenched dogma, but one that just might be founded upon a misunderstanding of scripture. What does the bible say about magic? It is commonly supposed that the bible clearly opposes magic. Certainly, there are portions of scripture that do seem to oppose magic, however, that may not be the full story. We will examine these and other instances in scripture to attempt to discover an accurate perspective of magic as presented in the bible.

Magic And Sin

Magic is sin. We ought not to get involved with anyone who practices magic. This is a commonly held view among Christianity. In fact, it is often taken even further to the degree that many Christians are afraid to even think about magic. If magic crops up in a book or a movie, they will just as soon avoid the content, condemn the author, and even persecute its fans. If a fellow Christian practices any type of mysticism, his actions may be labelled as magical, and the supposed "brother in Christ" may be rebuked, reviled, punished, or even excommunicated. Is this really a biblical perspective? Ought the children of the most high to live in fear of stories? Are we truly expected to eschew anything that might not fit conveniently into the small models of purely rationalist reasoning? Is God to be approached in an intellectual manner? Something seems amiss. And yet, there appears to be a biblical basis for this belief. It is undeniable that the bible contains several warnings and even prohibitions against magic. Let us begin by acknowledging several seemingly obvious passages:

- Deuteronomy 18:14-15 - *The nations you will dispossess listen to those who practice sorcery or divination. But as for you, the Lord your God has not permitted you to do so.*
- Leviticus 19:26 - *Do not practice divination or seek omens.*
- Leviticus 19:31 - *Do not turn to mediums or seek out spiritists, for you will be defiled by them. I am the Lord your God.*
- Leviticus 20:6 - *I will set my face against anyone who turns to mediums and spiritists to prostitute themselves by following them, and I will cut them off from their people.*
- Leviticus 20:27 - *A man or woman who is a medium or spiritist among you must be put to death. You are to stone them; their blood will be on their own heads.*

At first glance these verses all seem quite clear. The bible commands against the sin of sorcery, or at the bare minimum, advises against getting involved with sorcery. But could this truly be the whole story? Or could it somehow be more complex?

In the next chapter, I'm going to jump to an opposite extreme for a while, so please bear with me while I attempt to make a point. Hopefully we will find some kind of more accurate assessment by the end of the book.

God Teaches Magic

Did you know that God taught Moses how to do magic spells? This occurs in Exodus chapter 4. Please feel free to read it in your own bible so you know I didn't edit it, then come back here and we'll walk through it.

Here is an abridged copy, with a few non-pertinent verses removed:

God teaches Moses to transform his staff into a snake (and back) - *2 Then the Lord said to [Moses], "What is that in your hand?" "A staff," he replied. 3 The Lord said, "Throw it on the ground." Moses threw it on the ground and it became a snake, and he ran from it. 4 Then the Lord said to him, "Reach out your hand and take it by the tail." So Moses reached out and took hold of the snake and it turned back into a staff in his hand. 5 "This," said the Lord, "is so that they may believe that the Lord, the God of their fathers—the God of Abraham, the God of Isaac and the God of Jacob—has appeared to you."*

God teaches Moses to cause and cure leprosy - *6 Then the Lord said, "Put your hand inside your cloak." So Moses put his hand into his cloak, and when he took it out, the skin was leprous — it had become as white as snow. 7 "Now put it back into your cloak," he said. So Moses put his hand back into his cloak, and when he took it out, it was restored, like the rest of his flesh.*

God teaches Moses to transform water to blood - *8 Then the Lord said, "If they do not believe you or pay attention to the first sign, they may believe the second. 9 But if they do not believe these two signs or listen to you, take some water from the Nile and pour it on the dry ground. The water you take from the river will become blood on the ground."*

God promises to help, but commands Moses to perform the signs - *14 Then the Lord's anger burned against Moses and he said, "What about your brother, Aaron the Levite? I know he can speak well. He is already on his way to meet you, and he will be glad to see you. 15 You shall speak to him and put words in his mouth;* ***I will help both of you speak and will teach you what to do.*** *16 He will speak to the people for you, and it will be as if he were your mouth and as if you were God to him. 17 But* ***take this staff in your hand so you can perform the signs with it****."*

God gives Moses the power - *21 The Lord said to Moses, "When you return to Egypt,* ***see that you perform before Pharaoh all the wonders I have given you the power to do.*** *But I will harden his heart so that he will not let the people go. 22 Then say to Pharaoh, 'This is what the Lord says: Israel is my firstborn son, 23 and I told you, "Let my son go, so he may worship me." But you refused to let him go; so I will kill your firstborn son.'"*

Moses affirms God's command - *27 The Lord said to Aaron, "Go into the wilderness to meet Moses." So he* *met Moses at the mountain of God and kissed him. 28 Then Moses told Aaron everything the Lord had sent him to say, and also about* ***all the signs he had commanded him to perform.***

Moses performs the signs - *29 Moses and Aaron brought together all the elders of the Israelites, 30 and Aaron told them everything the Lord had said to Moses.* ***He also performed the signs before the people, 31 and they believed.*** *And when they heard that the Lord was concerned about them and had seen their misery, they bowed down and worshiped.*

So, to summarize:

Step 1 - God teaches Moses three spells
Spell #1: **Transform a Staff to a Snake**
How to do it: throw it on the ground to trigger the transformation, and pick it up by the tail to reverse it
Spell #2: **Create and Cure Leprosy**
How to do it: by sticking his hand into his jacket
Spell #3: **Transform Water into Blood**
How to do it: by pouring some river water onto the ground

Step 2 - God explains why Moses needs these spells: so that the Hebrews may believe that their God truly appeared to Moses - to give Moses credibility.

So far so good. But there is more to the process. Let's look at the rest of the steps.

Step 3 - God promises to help Moses
Step 4 - God commands Moses to perform the signs
Step 5 - God gives Moses the power to perform the signs
Step 6 - Moses accepts the task and testifies about it to his brother
Step 7 - Moses performs the tasks

Wait a minute. Actually, I added a step which isn't really present in the Bible? Can you spot it? Look at verse 21:

21 The Lord said to Moses, "When you return to Egypt, see that you perform before Pharaoh all the wonders I ***have given you the power*** *to do.*

God uses the past tense. I have already given you the power to do these things. Step 5 doesn't belong here. There is no step where God actually gives Moses the power. God doesn't do anything specific to literally give Moses power.

This can't be right, can it? Go read the chapter again in your own bible. Can you find a spot where God gives Moses power in the present tense? No? Why? Because, He has already given it to him.

Moses has the power to do it because God taught him HOW to do it. God taught him HOW, and that action included the power.

- Throw the stick on the ground to make a snake.

- Stick your hand in your jacket to make it leprous.
- Pour the water on the ground to make it blood.

The Action is the power. The act of performing the rite is the power of the spell. This is not some request to God to step in and do something, this is a man performing the exact steps which themselves cause the outcome. This is a spell.

Miracles Or Magic

Moses learned how to perform specific actions that caused certain impossible events to happen. God calls these events "signs" because they are intended as a sign of credibility for Moses to show to the Hebrews.

They may also be called miracles. For all intents and purposes we could also call them "spells". This is a pretty clear example of God commanding and teaching what appears to be magic.

I'm sure that some people will object to the nomenclature here. They will point out that miracles are not magic. So what exactly is the difference between miracles and magic?

When trying to find a difference, the first thing that came to my mind is that of source. That miracles are from God and magic is not. Another thought is that miracles are DONE BY God. Well, there is a difference between miracles and magic. So let's look at the differences.

Magic is often defined as "the power of apparently influencing the course of events by using mysterious or supernatural forces."[1] Impossible events that actually happen can certainly be considered "mysterious" and "supernatural" and whatever unknown or unexplained

---

[1] Lexico.com

force that is behind them is therefore also mysterious and supernatural.

Miracles are defined as "a surprising and welcome event that is not explicable by natural or scientific laws and is therefore considered to be the work of a divine agency."

Both miracles and magic are unexplained and unexpected events, outside the typical cause and effect of normal physical laws. In the case of miracles, as opposed to magic, a divine source is assumed.

	Impossible?	**Performed By**
Magic	Yes	not specified
Miracles	Yes	God

Both magic and miracles perform impossible actions. The difference is that if God does it, it is called a miracle. However, as Exodus clearly states, the source of the signs performed by Moses was actually Moses, not God. To be clear, yes God instigated the idea, and he provided Moses with both power and knowledge. But it was up to Moses to actually go and DO the work; perform the signs, work the magic. With this in mind, the "magic" definition actually fits better than the "miracle" definition.

Miracles are things that God does. In this case, God didn't do it, so how can it be a miracle?

Moses' experience was decidedly NOT a case of "DONE BY God". Rather, God specifically and blatantly teaches Moses to do the stuff. God expects and commands and empowers Moses to do it. The miracles are DONE BY Moses. So does that mean they are not miracles?

This is not a man asking God to work (prayer), it's God teaching a man to work. This is not God overcoming the laws of physics. This is Moses working within the systems that God has made and doing something that would normally be considered impossible.

The bible consistently teaches that nothing is impossible, not just for God, but for people who follow God. God promises numerous times that his followers will do impossible acts.

Whether you call them miracles or magic, the bible condones, expects, and promises "impossible acts" done by men.

Magic As Sin: Revisited

Let's go back to the passage we started with, in Deuteronomy 18. This time we'll read a bit more of the context

The nations you will dispossess ***listen to those who practice sorcery or divination****. But as for you, the Lord your* ***God has not permitted you to do so****. The Lord your God will raise up for you* ***a prophet*** *like me from among you, from your fellow Israelites.* ***You must listen to*** *him. For this is what you asked of the Lord your God at Horeb on the day of the assembly when you said, "Let us not hear the voice of the Lord our God nor see this great fire anymore, or we will die." The Lord said to me: "What they say is good. I will raise up for them a prophet like you from among their fellow Israelites, and I will put my words in his mouth. He will tell them everything I command him. I myself will call to account anyone who does not listen to my words that the prophet speaks in my name. But a prophet who presumes to speak in my name anything I have not commanded, or a prophet who speaks in the name of other gods, is to be put to death." You may say to yourselves, "How can we know when a message has not been spoken by the Lord?" If what a prophet proclaims in the name of the Lord does not take place or come true, that is a message the Lord has not spoken. That prophet has spoken presumptuously, so do not be alarmed.*

Deuteronomy 18 Summary:

1. God sent Moses as a prophet to Israel (v 15)
2. God will choose more prophets from among the Israelites.
3. Prophets are needed because the Israelites specifically asked God not to talk to them directly (v 16)
4. **You must listen to the prophets**
5. You are accountable to God if you do not listen (v 17)
6. Prophets are accountable to God for what they say
7. Sometimes prophets are wrong. Don't worry about it. That's not your problem. (v 22)
8. Other nations may get insight from sorcerers. Don't do that. You have prophets.

It turns out that this passage is not really about sorcery. It's actually about prophecy.

God gave the nation of Israel a special gift in the form of prophets. He did not give prophets to other nations as far as we know. The narrator of this passage (presumably Moses) claims to be a prophet (verse 15, "a prophet like me") and points out that the Lord has promised to send more prophets. The interesting point here though, is that the gift of prophets is already a compromise. What do I mean by this? Look at verse 16. God sends prophets because he made a deal with Israel. They asked him to back off a bit and the prophet was a way to do this.

Originally, God led his people out of slavery in Egypt, and he came to them personally. He literally showed up in the presence of the whole nation, atop the mountain, in a glorious cloud that everyone could see and hear. And the people didn't like it. God was too intense for them. They couldn't handle his glory and they rejected his holiness.

But God wanted to talk to his children! So God agreed to speak through a prophet, even though he could see a couple of likely issues with this scenario. Prophets are a lot easier to ignore right? And prophets are people who are prone to their own errors of judgement. But, for the sake of his children, He was willing to go easy on them by speaking through a prophet.

So the prophet is God's way of speaking to the people. And this is a special situation for the nation of Israel. The other nations of the area did not have this luxury. They had no ability to hear from God, for he had not given them prophets. If they wanted insight into the heavenly realm they practiced sorcery or divination. They found a way to contact other spiritual entities.

So the reason that sorcery and divination are sin is the same reason adultery is sin. Sorcery and divination are cheap imitations of God's gift of prophecy. Why seek answers from the dead, or from angelic or demonic beings, when the Creator, your loving Father, is right here wanting to talk to you and listen to you about every little thing? Talk about a slap in the face!

The analogy of adultery is apt, and follows through to a conclusion. Adultery is sin but sex is not. Sex is designed by God for a specific marriage relationship. Likewise, the fact that divination is a sin, does not make magic a sin. If you read Leviticus 18, you will see a long list of rules around sex. You may get the impression that sex is "bad", but this is in no way the intent. Rather, these rules are intended for avoiding bad decisions in sexuality, particularly in the areas of who is an appropriate partner. (ie. avoiding close family members, etc.).

In the same way, Leviticus' rules for magic ought to be seen in a framework of avoiding bad decisions in magic. Neither sex, nor magic are condemned broadly.

	Created By	**Good?**	**Certain Boundaries Specified?**
Sex	God	Yes	Yes
Magic	God	Yes	Yes

The bible presents God as the creator of all things. The earth, mankind, life, sex, magic, and everything else.

Colossians 1:16 - *For in him all things were created: things in heaven and on earth, visible and invisible, whether thrones or powers or rulers or authorities; all things have been created through him and for him.*

Revelation 4:11 - *Thou art worthy, O Lord, to receive glory and honour and power: for thou hast created all things, and for thy pleasure they are and were created.*

But remember, at the beginning of this article we listed five verses in Leviticus that condemn sorcery, and so far, we have only looked at one in depth. Are these other verses also being misinterpreted? Let's take a closer look.

Leviticus 19:26 - *Do not practice divination or seek omens.*

Leviticus 19:31 - *Do not turn to mediums or seek out spiritists, for you will be defiled by them. I am the Lord your God.*

Leviticus 20:6 - *I will set my face against anyone who turns to mediums and spiritists to prostitute themselves by following them, and I will cut them off from their people.*

Leviticus 20:27 - *A man or woman who is a medium or spiritist among you must be put to death. You are to stone them; their blood will be on their own heads.*

Interestingly, all of these verses are actually very specific in terms of what the exact issue is. In each case, it is the idea of consulting mediums or spiritists. A medium is one who consults the dead, while a spiritist is one who consults other spiritual entities. Both of these practices fall into the category of seeking knowledge from beyond. So, actually, yes, these other verses are in fact in line with the Deuteronomy passage. God has already provided a way for us to seek knowledge from him, through prophecy, a relationship based intimacy of God that leads to divinely inspired knowledge and wisdom. Moses was one of these prophets and there have been many others throughout biblical history, and on down to our current situation where Christ has made a way for all men to partake in that type of intimate relationship with God and experience the prophetic gift for themselves. This was the way God designed and intended man to hear from him in the garden of Eden and all throughout the bible. This is the only reason that mediums and spiritists are condemned. Their actions are akin to adultery and prostitution. They replace God with a cheap imitation devoid of divine relationship, seeking only a quick answer to the problem at hand.

When Moses gave the law to the people of Israel, it initially included the book of Leviticus. Later, Moses added the book of Deuteronomy. Both these books are ostensibly written by Moses and given to the hebrew nation after their exodus from Egypt.

Back in Egypt, the people had witnessed Moses perform magic. He changed his staff into a snake, he caused and cured leprosy, he turned water to blood. He also summoned swarms of locusts, and lice. He created boils, and unnatural darkness for three days.

We should note that Moses did not perform all the plagues himself. Some were performed by Moses, but it would appear that for some plagues, Moses was acting as prophet, stating what God himself would do. It was God, not Moses, who created the frogs, lightning, hail, diseased livestock, and death of the firstborn sons.

Moses was well-known to have performed these magic deeds. Moses was the leader of the entire nation. There was not a single person in the nation who did not know that Moses practiced magic. There would be no possibility of interpreting the laws given by Moses as a condemnation of magic.

And Moses' status as a magi was not merely a past that he no longer lived. He continued to actively practice magic throughout the period of the exodus and the wandering in the desert. This continued after the law was given. If the law condemned magic, the people would have been required to stone Moses to death.

Deuteronomy 34:10-12 clearly states that it was Moses, not God who performed this magic.

Since then, no prophet has risen in Israel like ***Moses,*** *whom the Lord knew face to face,* ***who did all those signs and wonders the Lord sent him to do*** *in Egypt — to Pharaoh and to all his officials and to his whole land.* ***For no one has ever shown the mighty power or performed the awesome deeds that Moses did*** *in the sight of all Israel.*

The Witch of Endor

I do not want to leave any stone unturned in this investigation. There is another well-known verse in 1 Samuel, that appears to condemn magic. Let's take a look.

1 Samuel 28 tells the story of King Saul and the witch of Endor.

Now Samuel was dead, and all Israel had mourned for him and buried him in his own town of Ramah. ***Saul had expelled the mediums and spiritists from the land.***

...When Saul saw the Philistine army, he was afraid; terror filled his heart. ***He inquired of the Lord, but the Lord did not answer him by dreams or Urim or prophets****. Saul then said to his attendants, "***Find me a woman who is a medium****, so I may go and inquire of her." "There is one in Endor," they said.*

*So Saul disguised himself, putting on other clothes, and at night he and two men went to the woman. "***Consult a spirit for me," he said, "and bring up for me the one I name****." But the woman said to him, "***Surely you know what Saul has done. He has cut off the mediums and spiritists from the land****. Why have you set a trap for my life to bring about my death?" Saul swore to her by the Lord, "As surely as the Lord lives, you will not be punished for this."*

*Then the woman asked, "Whom shall I bring up for you?" "**Bring up Samuel,**" he said. When the woman saw Samuel, she cried out at the top of her voice and said to Saul, "Why have you deceived me? You are Saul!" The king said to her, "Don't be afraid. What do you see?" The woman said, "I see a ghostly figure coming up out of the earth." "What does he look like?" he asked. "An old man wearing a robe is coming up," she said. Then Saul knew it was Samuel, and he bowed down and prostrated himself with his face to the ground.* ***Samuel said to Saul, "Why have you disturbed me by bringing me up?"***

"I am in great distress," Saul said. "The Philistines are fighting against me, and ***God has departed from me. He no longer answers me, either by prophets or by dreams. So I have called on you to tell me what to do****."*

Samuel said, "Why do you consult me, ***now that the Lord has departed from you and become your enemy?*** *The Lord has done what he predicted through me. The Lord has torn the kingdom out of your hands and given it to one of your neighbors—to David. Because you did not obey the Lord or carry out his fierce wrath against the Amalekites, the Lord has done this to you today. The Lord will deliver both Israel and you into the hands of the Philistines, and tomorrow you and your sons will be with me. The Lord will also give the army of Israel into the hands of the Philistines."*

Once again I'll summarize:

1. The Prophet Samuel is dead. (He always gave Saul bad news, anyway)
2. Another prophet has not yet been appointed. (who wants more bad news?)
3. There were no diviners, sorcerers, and mediums around.
    - Saul had expelled them from the land. (or did he?)
    - Why did he do that? Because God told him to.
4. Saul had a problem and needed an answer from God
5. God didn't answer (v 6)
    - Because Saul did not obey God (v 16-18, see also 1 Sam 15)
    - Because Saul did not listen to the prophet Samuel.
    - Because Saul actively opposed God[3)]
6. Saul finds one of the supposedly evicted mediums to speak to Samuel from beyond the grave.
7. Samuel's ghost tells Saul why God has not answered Saul
8. Samuel's ghost foretells Saul's death the following day.

This story serves to back up the previous conclusion. Don't consult mediums. Rather, listen to the prophets.

Saul got himself into a giant mess because he purposefully ignored the words of the prophets. Then he tried to hire someone who might tell him what he wanted to hear. It is interesting though, that the medium herself does not appear to incur the wrath of God. We know that Saul had expelled the mediums from the land. Presumably, this was because God had told him to do so, in order to purge the land of their wickedness. The trouble here is that that is entirely presumption. The bible does not relate any such communication between God and Saul. In fact, as this passage clearly states, Saul was unable to hear from God, and God seemed to ignore Saul's prayers. So perhaps Saul's purging of the mediums from the land was not actually a godly plan. It's entirely possible that the whole scheme was a way to get rid of Samuel and the other godly prophets. In any case, the supposed "Witch of Endor" is not condemned, or even accused of any wrongdoing. She simply acts according to her talents, and everyone seems to be fine with that. The only person incurring any wrath here is Saul.

The Godly Magic Of Moses

Let us return to the story of Moses. We have already seen many examples of his magic. Many times Moses performed magic, usually at the request of God and with some instruction from God. Aside from the instances we already looked at, Moses also parted the red sea[4)], cleansed bitter waters to make them drinkable[5)], and brought forth water from a rock[6)7)]. He healed the people using a bronze snake[8)]. These things were all done in order to provide for the community. We'll look at the bronze snake further in a later chapter.

The water from a rock example is an interesting one though. It seems as though the story occurs twice, but it is actually two separate incidents that take place nearly forty years apart with only a few differences. Much has been written about these two stories, generally focusing on the question of why Moses was punished in the second instance. I can add nothing to this particular discussion. Rather, I will limit my comments to the magic part of the stories. What can we glean from this?

Exodus 17 - at the beginning of their desert journey	Numbers 20 - near the end of their desert journey
The whole Israelite community set out from the Desert of Sin, traveling from place to place as the Lord commanded. They camped at Rephidim, but there was no water for the people to drink. 2 So they quarreled with Moses and said, "Give us water to drink." *Moses replied, "Why do you quarrel with me? Why do you put the Lord to the test?" 3 But the people were thirsty for water there, and they grumbled against Moses. They said, "Why did you bring us up out of Egypt to make us and our children and livestock die of thirst?"*	*In the first month the whole Israelite community arrived at the Desert of Zin, and they stayed at Kadesh. There Miriam died and was buried. 2 Now there was no water for the community, and the people gathered in opposition to Moses and Aaron.* *3 They quarreled with Moses and said, "If only we had died when our brothers fell dead before the Lord! 4 Why did you bring the Lord's community into this wilderness, that we and our livestock should die here? 5 Why did you bring us up out of Egypt to this terrible place? It has no grain or figs, grapevines or pomegranates. And there is no water to drink!"*

4 Then Moses cried out to the Lord, "What am I to do with these people? They are almost ready to stone me." *5 The Lord answered Moses, "Go out in front of the people. Take with you some of the elders of Israel and take in your hand the staff with which you struck the Nile, and go. 6* ***I will stand there before you by the rock*** *at Horeb.* ***Strike the rock****, and water will come out of it for the people to drink."*	*6 Moses and Aaron went from the assembly to the entrance to the tent of meeting and fell facedown, and the glory of the Lord appeared to them. 7 The Lord said to Moses, 8 "Take the staff, and you and your brother Aaron gather the assembly together.* ***Speak to that rock*** *before their eyes and it will pour out its water. You will bring water out of the rock for the community so they and their livestock can drink."*
So Moses did this in the sight of the elders of Israel. 7 And he called the place Massah[a] and Meribah[b] because the Israelites quarreled and because they tested the Lord saying, "Is the Lord ***among us*** *or not?"*	*9 So Moses took the staff from the Lord's presence, just as he commanded him. 10 He and Aaron gathered the assembly together in front of the rock and Moses said to them, "Listen, you rebels, must we bring you water out of this rock?" 11 Then Moses raised his arm and struck the rock twice with his staff. Water gushed out, and the community and their livestock drank.*

We see that in terms of magic spells, these two events use two different spells with similar results. Or rather, Moses was supposed to use two different spells. On the later occasion, it seems God wanted to teach Moses a new spell; a more powerful spell perhaps. One that caused the water to flow using only the sound of his voice. Instead, Moses fell back on the old tried and true spell, which required the physical action and energy of striking the rock with his staff. Could this be the reason he was punished by God following this incident? Was it because he refused to learn—refused to grow? Was he resting on his laurels and becoming lazy? Was he, for some unknown reason, avoiding the continued blessings that God had in store for him? I don't know, and I'm certainly not trying to disparage the revered patriarch, but clearly he did something wrong, and folks have been trying to sort out what it was ever since. Is it possible that using the wrong spell for the job was Moses' downfall?

Moses vs. the Egyptian Sorcerers

Most of the cases we have examined so far have involved God commanding, giving instructions, and possibly granting power to his followers to perform the magic.

What about other cases where the power was not given directly by God? Is it possible for magical power to originate from some ungodly source? Are there any instances of this in the bible? Is it possible to choose to perform magical acts by different sources? Can one act by either God's power or by some other power source?

Let's turn back to Moses' rise to leadership, and re-examine his relation to the Egyptian sorcerers.

The story of Moses and his brother Aaron vs. Pharaoh's mages, as presented in Exodus 7, appears to follow a classic archetype of good versus evil. It could be summed up with Moses declaring and proving that "My righteous magic is better than your evil magic!" But there is just one slight problem with this view. The magic is the same. Look at verse 11 and 22 of chapter 7, and verse 7 of chapter 8. Three times, we see the same phrase: "the Egyptian magicians also did the same things by their secret arts". The phrase is repeated three times; once for each of the first three plagues: the snake, the blood, the frogs.

On the other hand, the phrase "by their secret arts" actually does seem to imply that perhaps their techniques differed from Moses'. This may be evidence for the "God's power vs Satan's power" view.

The gnats and the flies could not be reproduced by Pharaoh's mages. Neither could the livestock plague, the boils, or the hail. Nor the locusts, or the darkness.

There are a couple of different conclusions one could draw:

1. Moses' magic was different from the mages' because it originated from a different, and presumably better or stronger source.
2. Moses was simply "better" or "stronger" than the mages. This does not necessarily imply anything about source.

How might we determine which conclusion is more accurate? Can we infer an answer to the question of source?

There is an important clue given by Jesus that may be applicable here. Jesus is asked essentially this same question. The Pharisees accuse him of casting out demons by the power of Beelzebub, lord of demons. Jesus replies, "A kingdom divided cannot stand". This story is related in two of the gospels. It can be found in both Mark 3 and in Matthew 12. The two renditions are different enough to allow some interesting interpretive exercises.

In Mark 3 Jesus explains himself thoroughly. We look at the Mark explanation in the following section. However, in the book of Matthew, the story is given with a little more room for interpretation. Could it be that Matthew is purposely provoking us to think about different possible aspects of Jesus' comments. Could it be that the Mark explanation may not tell the whole story? Is there another possible aspect of the Matthew presentation? Could it be that Jesus was implying that there is only one way by which the universe works; only one system?

The Mark Explanation might be simplified and represented as follows:

"You cast out demons by Beelzebub." Said the Pharisees.

Jesus answered, "No I don't, because then Beelzebub would be dividing his own kingdom. Why would he do that?"

Mark 3 is very clear that this is at least one possible intended meaning. Jesus expounds upon this idea and furthers his analogy by talking about "binding the strong man". Clearly Jesus is speaking of his own authority over the demonic forces by way of defeating Satan through his death and resurrection (remember both Jesus and Satan are not bound by time the same way we are so even though Jesus' death had not yet occurred, the effects were already felt by the demonic kingdom)

There are a few radical implications of the Mark Explanation

1. Satan can perform miracles. (If he could not, this would have made a much stronger argument. Jesus would have said “No I don't, that's impossible, since Beelzebub can’t do miracles”)

2. Satan does perform miracles. (Same argument as above.)

3. Satan can cast out demons but that would be counterproductive for him.

One interesting aspect of this interpretation is that the logic depends on putting yourself in Satan’s shoes, the shoes of a lunatic. Why does Jesus ask us to do this? Does it even make sense to try? Why would Jesus put himself in these shoes? How can we know, and why would we want to try to know what Satan is thinking? Does anything he did ever make any sense? Satan is trying to overcome God, an utterly foolish proposition indeed.

Another point is that this perspective can easily breed fear. Jesus has bound the strong man. What about those of us living much later? It seems that the strong man may have broken loose. The devil is clearly alive and well on planet earth. So if he in fact has power, how do we know that even our own works are not fueled by demonic power? This is the same fear the Pharisees themselves must have felt. It is based on a lie of Satan trying to steal credit for Jesus' good work. When we believe that it is possible to work in Jesus' power OR Satan’s power, it casts doubt on everything. We must ask ourselves constantly, am I acting by Beelzebub? We also feel the need to "protect" each other from others who may be acting in Satan's power. This often results in our taking on the very words of the Pharisees themselves and accusing our own brothers and sisters in Christ of acting by Satan's power. We sling mud at other Christians just because we do not understand everything they say. All in all, the implications of this interpretation are decidedly unhealthy at best, and completely nonsensical at worst.

Matthew's telling of the story leaves room for interpretation. For example, here is a different slant on it:

"You cast out demons by Beelzebub." said the Pharisees.

Jesus replied, "It's a bogus question. The universe is not divided. How could it be? A divided kingdom cannot stand."

It does not make sense to talk of God's power or Satan's power because Satan has no power of his own. He is a created being, functioning inside God's universe. He merely uses his twisted will to misuse the inherent power built in to the universe by God's own design. Think about a crooked defense attorney pleading innocence on behalf of a guilty man. Does he use his own evil laws? No he uses THE laws. There is only one legal system. It is utilized by the just, and abused by the wicked. God made one, and only one set of laws for the universe to work under. It is complex. It can be manipulated for good or for wicked ends. We operate within it. Everything we do - even supernatural events fall under the overall system. The power is built into the operations of the universe. The physical laws are not all there is. There are spiritual principles that operate outside of space-time; these are also part of the one whole complex system.

- “The rain falls on the just and the unjust” - Matt 5:45
- The force of Gravity works the same way for everyone.
- The same nuclear forces are used for generating power and for bombing cities.
- There is not a separate set of forces for good and for evil.

So are Moses and the Pharaoh’s sorcerers tapping into the same force, from the same source? It would appear that this is in fact the case. Let's investigate another similar case with another great bible figure, one of Moses' ancestors, and the reason Moses and the Hebrews got to Egypt in the first place; Joseph.

Joseph & Egyptian Magic

Moses was not the first bible character to be trained in Egyptian magical arts. Around four hundred years earlier, as we read in Genesis 37, a young Canaanite man named Joseph had a gift from God to interpret dreams. This did not play to his favor at first, and he was soon sold by his brothers to a slave caravan bound for Egypt. In Egypt he was framed, fired, and imprisoned, but eventually, he found his way to the court of the pharaoh. Joseph tells the pharaoh, in Genesis 41:16, that he cannot interpret dreams of his own power but that "God will give Pharaoh the answer he desires."

Despite Joseph's humility, he easily interprets the dreams of the pharaoh. He does not need to pray to God for revelation. He again tells pharaoh "God has shown Pharaoh what he is about to do." and he simply translates the obvious symbology to Pharaoh. I say "obvious symbology" not because the symbols are obvious to you or I, but because they were clearly obvious to Joseph. Joseph did not see his gift as anything miraculous, magical, or even mysterious. Joseph felt that the mysterious part was in the dream itself. In his view, God planted coded information into the dreamer's mind. The act of interpreting the information was a straightforward process of decoding; more like the act of a translator who happened to be fluent in the two languages.

Eventually, Joseph landed a high ranking position in the Egyptian government due in large part to his supernatural abilities. To make a long story short, there are some shenanigans with his brothers, during which we see, in Genesis 44, two more references to Joseph's continued use of, in his own words, "divination". The story involves a silver cup, about which Joseph's steward remarks "Isn't this the cup my master drinks from and also uses for divination?" Joseph himself verifies this claim, asking his brothers, "Don't you know that a man like me can find things out by divination?"

How does the silver cup play into Joseph's methods? We don't know. He didn't seem to use any silver cups or any other objects in his early dream-interpretation days. What had changed? What was the extent of Joseph's later divination practices. We don't know. But it seems fairly safe to assume that they were not strictly limited to dream interpretation.

Daniel & Babylonian Magic

About fourteen hundred years after Joseph, we come across another story with a strangely familiar ring. Again, there is a young man, with a gift for dream interpretation. Again this young man finds himself in prison in a foreign land. This young man is named Daniel. And once again, we see Daniel, like Joseph, rise to a prominent position in the king's court, due to his dream interpretation skills. This time, the king is Nebuchadnezzar, ruler of the Babylonian empire.

According to the book of Daniel, Daniel had natural talents but was apparently trained in magic by the Babylonian priests, eventually becoming the High Priest of the Babylonian religion.

To these four young men [Daniel, and three companions] God gave knowledge and understanding of all kinds of literature and learning. And ***Daniel could understand visions and dreams of all kinds.***

Then the king ordered Ashpenaz, chief of his court officials, to bring into the king's service some of the Israelites from the royal family and the nobility—young men without any physical defect, handsome, ***showing aptitude for every kind of learning, well informed, quick to understand****, and qualified to serve in the king's palace. He was to teach them the language and literature of the Babylonians. The king assigned them a daily amount of food and wine from the king's table.*

They were to be ***trained for three years****, and after that they were to enter the king's service.*

At the end of the time set by the king to bring them into his service, the chief official presented them to Nebuchadnezzar. The king talked with them, and he ***found none equal to Daniel****, Hananiah, Mishael and Azariah; so they entered the king's service. In every matter of wisdom and understanding about which the king questioned them, he found them* ***ten times better than all the magicians and enchanters*** *in his whole kingdom.*

Just as Joseph did, Daniel gives credit to God for showing him the mysteries of the dreams, as we read in Daniel chapter 2:

During the night, the mystery was revealed to Daniel in a vision. Then Daniel praised the God of heaven and said:

*"****Praise be to the name of God*** *for ever and ever;wisdom and power are his.* ***He changes times and seasons****; he deposes kings and raises up others. He gives wisdom to the wise and knowledge to the discerning. He reveals deep and hidden things;* ***he knows what lies in darkness****, and light dwells with him. I thank and praise you, God of my ancestors: You have given me wisdom and power, you have made known to me what we asked of you, you have made known to us the dream of the king."*

Furthermore, Daniel explains to the king:

*Daniel replied, "***No wise man, enchanter, magician or diviner can explain to the king the mystery he has asked about***, but there is a God in heaven who reveals mysteries. He has shown King Nebuchadnezzar* ***what will happen in days to come***. *Your dream and the visions that passed through your mind as you were lying in bed are these:*

"As Your Majesty was lying there, ***your mind turned to things to come, and the revealer of mysteries showed you what is going to happen. As for me, this mystery has been revealed to me****, not because I have greater wisdom than anyone else alive, but so that Your Majesty may know the interpretation and that you may understand what went through your mind.*

Here, Daniel makes it even more clear than Joseph did, though they both shared a similar phenomenon, that the dreams of the king are actually a glimpse into a future time. The king and Daniel are experiencing prescient or precognitive visions. This is the realm of a special class of magicians known as soothsayers or fortune-tellers. We see, too, in Daniel chapter 4, that Daniel was promoted to the position of Chief Of The Magicians, and that his skill surpassed all of the other magicians in the king's court.

I, Nebuchadnezzar, was at home in my palace, contented and prosperous. I had a dream that made me afraid. As I was lying in bed, the images and visions that passed through my mind terrified me. So I commanded that all the wise men of Babylon be brought before me to interpret the dream for me. When ***the magicians, enchanters, astrologers and diviners*** *came, I told them the dream, but they could not interpret it for me. Finally, Daniel came into my presence and I told him the dream. (He is called Belteshazzar, after the name of my god, and the spirit of the holy gods is in him.) I said, "Belteshazzar,* ***chief of the magicians****, I know that* ***the spirit of the holy gods is in you****, and no mystery is too difficult for you.*

Daniel's position is validated even more explicitly in Daniel 5:11, which reads "King Nebuchadnezzar, appointed him chief of the magicians, enchanters, astrologers and diviners." Daniel was the greatest of the Babylonian magicians of his time. He was one of them. There is no indication that Daniel's methodologies or practices differed from those of the other magicians. Instead, what we see is a level of success as a result of divine favour. God blessed Daniel. God helped Daniel. This is what accounts for Daniel's expertise. God blessed Daniel as a practitioner of Babylonian magic.

Spells In The Law

Not only did God approve of Daniel's magic in his Babylonian cultural paradigm. God actually built magic into the core of Jewish culture, by way of one of the central components of Judaism. The Law, also known as The Torah. Christianity inherits this same law, and Jesus himself states "I have not come to abolish the law, but to fulfill it."

During Moses' tenure of leadership in the wilderness of Sinai, he set out a series of commandments and laws for the nation of Israel, that he received from God. Moses' magical upbringing found its way into this legal code. Most of us are familiar with the ten commandments, presented in Exodus 20. This is the extremely shortened version of Jewish law, but the full body of the law spans most of the books of Leviticus, and Deuteronomy, as well as significant portions of Exodus. This full legal code includes some strange and surprising contents.

One such example is found in Numbers 5:11-29 which describes a magic ritual involving a curse and a test, commanded by God to be used during trials of cases of adultery, to determine guilt or innocence of one suspected of "cheating". The passage is part of a lengthy legal section describing various offences and solutions. Most of them are quite straightforward, but this section is complicated by hidden evidence, and magic is prescribed to determine the truth. In other words, it's divination, which is defined as "the practice of seeking knowledge of the future or the unknown by supernatural means."

Then ***the Lord said*** *to Moses, "Speak to the Israelites and say to them: 'If a man's wife goes astray and is unfaithful to him so that another man has sexual relations with her, and* ***this is hidden*** *from her husband and her impurity* ***is undetected*** *(since there is* ***no witness*** *against her and she has* ***not been caught in the act****), and if feelings of jealousy come over her husband and* ***he suspects*** *his wife and she is impure—or if he is jealous and suspects her even though she is not impure— then he is to take his wife to the priest. He must also take an offering of a tenth of an ephah of barley flour on her behalf. He must not pour olive oil on it or put incense on it, because it is a grain offering for jealousy, a reminder-offering to draw attention to wrongdoing.*

" 'The priest shall bring her and have her stand before the Lord. Then ***he shall take some holy water in a clay jar and put some dust from the tabernacle floor into the water.*** *After the priest has had the woman stand before the Lord,* ***he shall loosen her hair and place in her hands the reminder-offering, the grain offering*** *for jealousy, while* ***he himself holds the bitter water*** *that brings a curse. Then the priest shall put the woman under oath and say to her, "If no other man has had sexual relations with you and you have not gone astray and become impure while married to your husband, may this bitter water that brings a curse not harm you. But if you have gone astray while married to your husband and you have made yourself impure by having sexual*

relations with a man other than your husband"—here ***the priest is to put the woman under this curse****—"may the Lord cause you to become a curse among your people when he makes your womb miscarry and your abdomen swell. May this water that brings a curse enter your body so that your abdomen swells or your womb miscarries."*

"'Then the woman is to say, "Amen. So be it."

"'The priest is to ***write these curses on a scroll and then wash them off into the bitter water. He shall make the woman drink the bitter water that brings a curse****, and this water that brings a curse and causes bitter suffering will enter her. The priest is to take from her hands the grain offering for jealousy, wave it before the Lord and bring it to the altar. The priest is then to take a handful of the grain offering as a memorial offering and burn it on the altar; after that, he is to have the woman drink the water. If she has made herself impure and been unfaithful to her husband, this will be the result: When she is made to drink the water that brings a curse and causes bitter suffering, it will enter her, her abdomen will swell and her womb will miscarry, and she will become a curse. If, however, the woman has not made herself impure, but is clean, she will be cleared of guilt and will be able to have children.*

This is about the most obvious description of sorcery as you can get. The priest is to mix up a magic potion which will cause a magic curse if the woman is guilty as charged. This sounds like a scene straight out of

Grimm's Fairy Tales. This potion is not simply some kind of medicinal cure. Medicine works regardless of guilt. This is unquestionably a magic spell.

The law contains many more examples of curses, though most of them do not come with the same explicit references to potions and spellcasting.

Blessings And Curses In The Law

Much of the book of Deuteronomy is focused on the laws that God gave to the nation of Israel through Moses. There are all kinds of commands and legal processes described in the book, and it all is tied together with blessings and curses. Similar to the magic potion discussed in the previous section, we see that there are consequences which will automatically occur, depending on the actions of the nation. If the people are diligent in following the law, then good things will happen—they will be blessed. If, on the other hand, the people choose to disobey the law, they will be sure to face all kinds of calamitous results, for they shall be cursed.

Deuteronomy chapter 11 introduces the law and chapter 28 sums it up. Between the two chapters a wide variety of laws are detailed. In both chapters we find the whole body of the law wrapped up and encapsulated within a blessing and a curse. Those who follow the law will be blessed and those who disobey will be cursed.

*"**You shall therefore keep the whole commandment that I command you today**, that you may be strong, and go in and take possession of the land that you are going over to possess, and that you may live long in the land that the Lord swore to your fathers to give to them and to their offspring, a land flowing with milk and honey.*

"And if you will indeed obey my commandments that I command you today, to love the Lord your God, and to serve him with all your heart and with all your soul, he

will give the rain for your land in its season, the early rain and the later rain, that you may gather in your grain and your wine and your oil. And he will give grass in your fields for your livestock, and you shall eat and be full. Take care lest your heart be deceived, and you turn aside and serve other gods and worship them; then the anger of the Lord will be kindled against you, and he will shut up the heavens, so that there will be no rain, and the land will yield no fruit, and you will perish quickly off the good land that the Lord is giving you.

*"**See, I am setting before you today a blessing and a curse: the blessing, if you obey the commandments of the Lord your God, which I command you today, and the curse, if you do not obey** the commandments of the Lord your God, but turn aside from the way that I am commanding you today, to go after other gods that you have not known.*

The blessing will be upon all the people if they as a nation obey the laws as outlined. They will have land, military victory, good weather, and good crops.

Chapter 28 goes into more detail about the results of the blessing, and especially about the curse.

*"**And if you faithfully obey the voice of the Lord your God**, being careful to do all his commandments that I command you today, the Lord your God will set you high above all the nations of the earth. And **all these blessings shall come upon you** and overtake you, if you obey the voice of the Lord your God. Blessed shall you*

be in the city, and blessed shall you be in the field. Blessed shall be the fruit of your womb and the fruit of your ground and the fruit of your cattle, the increase of your herds and the young of your flock. Blessed shall be your basket and your kneading bowl. Blessed shall you be when you come in, and blessed shall you be when you go out.

"The Lord will cause your enemies who rise against you to be defeated before you. They shall come out against you one way and flee before you seven ways. The Lord will command the blessing on you in your barns and in all that you undertake. And he will bless you in the land that the Lord your God is giving you. The Lord will establish you as a people holy to himself, as he has sworn to you, if you keep the commandments of the Lord your God and walk in his ways. And all the peoples of the earth shall see that you are called by the name of the Lord, and they shall be afraid of you. And the Lord will make you abound in prosperity, in the fruit of your womb and in the fruit of your livestock and in the fruit of your ground, within the land that the Lord swore to your fathers to give you. The Lord will open to you his good treasury, the heavens, to give the rain to your land in its season and to bless all the work of your hands. And you shall lend to many nations, but you shall not borrow. And the Lord will make you the head and not the tail, and you shall only go up and not down, if you obey the commandments of the Lord your God, which I command you today, being careful to do them, and if you do not turn aside from any of the words that I command you

today, to the right hand or to the left, to go after other gods to serve them.

Curses for Disobedience

*"**But if you will not obey the voice of the Lord your God or be careful to do all his commandments and his statutes that I command you today, then all these curses shall come upon you** and overtake you. Cursed shall you be in the city, and cursed shall you be in the field. Cursed shall be your basket and your kneading bowl. Cursed shall be the fruit of your womb and the fruit of your ground, the increase of your herds and the young of your flock. Cursed shall you be when you come in, and cursed shall you be when you go out.*

*"The Lord will send on you **curses, confusion, and frustration in all that you undertake to do, until you are destroyed** and perish quickly on account of the evil of your deeds, because you have forsaken me. The Lord will make the **pestilence** stick to you until he has consumed you off the land that you are entering to take possession of it. The Lord will strike you with **wasting disease** and with **fever, inflammation and fiery heat**, and with **drought and with blight and with mildew**. They shall pursue you until you perish. And the heavens over your head shall be bronze, and the earth under you shall be iron. **The Lord will make the rain of your land powder. From heaven dust shall come down on you until you are destroyed.***

"The Lord will cause you to be ***defeated before your enemies****. You shall go out one way against them and flee seven ways before them. And* ***you shall be a horror to all the kingdoms of the earth****. And your dead body shall be food for all birds of the air and for the beasts of the earth, and there shall be no one to frighten them away. The Lord will strike you with* ***the boils of Egypt, and with tumors and scabs and itch, of which you cannot be healed****. The Lord will strike you with* ***madness and blindness and confusion*** *of mind, and you shall grope at noonday, as the blind grope in darkness, and* ***you shall not prosper in your ways****. And you shall be only* ***oppressed and robbed continually****, and there shall be* ***no one to help you****.*

It goes on and on. We'll skip a page or two, to get to the wrap up.

*"****All these curses shall come upon you and pursue you and overtake you till you are destroyed, because you did not obey the voice of the Lord your God, to keep his commandments and his statutes that he commanded you****.*

God has placed a terrible curse upon his followers. This curse is tightly bound to the laws proclaimed through Moses. In fact, there is only one way out of said curse, and that is to obey the attached laws.

Blessings And Curses Of The Patriarchs

These curses and blessings did not begin with Moses. Moses came from a long line of magic users. Long before Moses' time, the patriarchs; Abraham, Isaac, and Jacob engaged in magic use by way of invoking blessings and curses.

Typically, this occurred in the context of a familial blessing being passed on from a father to a son, generally while the father was on his deathbed. We see several examples of this phenomenon in the book of Genesis, where we follow the lineage of Abraham, his son Isaac, grandson Jacob, and great-grandson Judah. Their particular story begins with the blessing of Abraham. As we read in Genesis chapter 12:

The Lord had said to Abram, "Go from your country, your people and your father's household to the land I will show you. I will make you into a great nation, and I will bless you; I will make your name great, and you will be a blessing. I will bless those who bless you, and whoever curses you I will curse; and all peoples on earth will be blessed through you."

It is worth noting that this blessing comes in the midst of a failed migration. The previous chapter reveals that Abraham's father, Terah, took his family and together they set out from the city of Ur, in today's Turkey, upon whose outskirts the ancient site of Gobekli Tepe is situated, "to go to Canaan." But when they came to Harran, about forty miles south, they settled there. They never made it to their intended destination. Not even close. They barely made it over the county line. They ended up settling down in the neighboring district, a vacant area which Terah named "Harran", after his father Haran, and there they stayed for many years. Thus, when Abraham is blessed, part of the blessing is a renewal of his father's original dream of reaching Canaan. We don't know why Terah wanted to go there. There is no evidence that there was any sort of divine direction to do so. There is no judgement from God when he compromised his vision and stayed in Haran instead. There was undoubtedly some good reason to stay there. Yet it seems that the original family dream never completely died, and eventually his son Abraham took up the torch, so to speak.

So the blessing of Abraham has less to do with God telling him where to go, and more to do with Abraham fulfilling a familial obligation. I imagine that Terah never stopped talking about how cool it was going to be "when we finally go to Canaan" and that Abraham hearing his father's longing, became enamored with the dream himself. We tend to think that Abraham had some divinely appointed manifest destiny. Could it simply be that he wanted to do right by his father and fulfil the family dream?

At any rate, God himself apparently did bless Abraham, essentially saying to him "I'm with you in this plan, and I've got your back." However, Abraham still didn't go to

Canaan. And again, God didn't have a problem with that. Abraham spends the next few years going briefly THROUGH Canaan, but moving on to the Negev desert, then to Egypt, then back to the Negev, and finally into the region of Canaan. We don't know why he kept wandering around. But we do know that managed to get into a fair bit of mischief along the way. Particularly, while visiting Egypt:

The Lord inflicted serious diseases on Pharaoh and his household because of Abram's wife Sarai. So Pharaoh summoned Abram. "What have you done to me?"(Genesis 12:17)

Here we see a curse at work. Abraham, by now a fairly prominent businessman, was able to meet with the Pharaoh (essentially the king). It didn't hurt his bargaining position that he happened to have a very beautiful "sister", (actually his wife) and soon they were successfully negotiating and conducting business, until lo and behold, things suddenly turned sour, and the Pharaoh and his whole family were struck with some kind of disease. Pharaoh puts two and two together, realizing that he had inadvertently slept with a married woman. The unintended actions of the Pharaoh somehow automatically kicked the curse into gear. Remember, God had already invoked the curse and blessing bundled together: "*I will bless those who bless you, and whoever curses you I will curse.*" The curse had already been enacted, enabled, and launched, and was simply waiting for someone to come along and disrespect Abraham. Abraham's stupid decision to push his wife into the king's bed was enough to trigger it.

A few chapters later, Abraham is now well settled into the land of Canaan, and has essentially become a tribal chief. He eventually gets roped into local skirmishes and ends up becoming a war hero, after defeating the despotic warlord, Kedorlaomer. Bera king of Sodom, Birsha king of Gomorrah, and a couple other kings, had joined forces in a rebellion against the high king Kedorlaomer king of Elam, and his allies, most likely over issues with Kedorlaomer's taxation policies.

After putting down the rebellion, Kedorlaomer's army went rampaging throughout the land to crush any further uprisings before they might begin. defeating the several other tribes including Amalekites, and the Amorites.

But the original rebels rallied a comeback and launched a second campaign against Kedorlaomer and were routed a second time. This defeat resulted in the capture of some of Abraham's relatives, at which point, Abraham decided it was time to get involved in the war. He summoned his own personal army of over three hundred trained fighters, to launch a nocturnal sneak attack, in which the mighty armies of Kedorlaomer were finally defeated.

Abraham was hailed as a war hero by the king of Sodom, and Melchizedek king of Salem, who blessed Abram, saying, *"Blessed be Abram by God Most High, Creator of heaven and earth. And praise be to God Most*

High, who delivered your enemies into your hand." Melchizedek is often credited for granting a great blessing upon Abraham. Essentially, though this may not be entirely accurate. Melchizedek simply observed and remarked upon the existing blessing upon Abraham and the curse upon his enemies.

Pre-Abrahamic Curses

Even before these great patriarchs of the faith, we see the use of blessings and curses. All the way back to the earliest stories, curses and blessings play an important role in the lives of the heroes of old.

Cain is cursed for murdering his brother, who was himself blessed by God. Enoch was blessed in a very unique way. Noah is the recipient of another special blessing, while his son Ham received a curse. And this is all to say nothing of the original blessings and curses which take place in the garden of Eden with Adam and Eve and the Serpent and the Tree Of the Knowledge Of Good And Evil. It is clear that back in the recesses of our most ancient stories, we see God invoking spells upon his people, and we see some spells that seem to simply flow directly from their actions or their interaction with various magical artifacts. The Tree Of the Knowledge Of Good And Evil is one such artifact that seems to represent some kind of magical power of its own. The tree embodies a powerful curse that falls on all of mankind. In many ways the tree itself may be considered some kind of magic item.

Much much more can and will be said regarding these particular stories, as they are richly multifaceted with significant archetypes, symbology, and wisdom. For now I will simply promise the reader that much more is to follow in my forthcoming books.

Jesus The Magician

Of course, no one figures more prominently in the Christian Bible than Jesus the Messiah, the Christ come to break the curse. It is said he was sent to earth from heaven to replace the ancient Edenic/Adamic curse with a new covenant—that he has come to bring, and in fact to be, a blessing to all of mankind. He is the blessed blesser.

With his words and his actions, he blessed. He declared many blessings in his famous sermon on the mount. Blessed are the merciful. Blessed are the meek. Blessed are those who hunger and thirst after righteousness, etc. His actions spoke louder than his words. They embodied blessing. He treated the downtrodden with respect and kindness. He gave generously. He healed. He gave sight to the blind. He caused the lame to walk. He gave strength to the weak and hope to the hopeless.

He performed miracles. He did many impossible actions. How did he do it? Perhaps it would be more accurate to ask what spells did he know? He could walk on water. He could walk through walls. He could disappear into thin air. He could cause matter to multiply or to appear from nowhere.

He turned water into wine. This is his first recorded spell. The mundane becomes the magic. Wine may symbolize an alternative perspective. The open gate. The magic elixir. Magical thought for everyone. The wedding guests drank feely and entered the way—Jesus offers all entry into the Kingdom of heaven.

The Magical Disciples

Jesus passed on his magical skills to his disciples. In Matthew 28 he tells his disciples, "*All authority in heaven and on earth has been given to me. Go therefore and make disciples of all nations, baptizing them in the name of the Father and of the Son and of the Holy Spirit, teaching them to observe all that I have commanded you.*"

Not only has he passed on his knowledge, but he commands his disciples to do likewise. He is using a "train the trainer" model. Reading the gospels, we may not immediately see that his followers actually learned much from him. They often exhibit doubt and confusion. Yet, in Luke 10, seventy of his disciples report their successful results in healing the sick and casting out demons, and similarly in Mark 9 it is clear that even those not in the inner circle had already picked up some tips from observing Jesus, and were working miracles.

As we read on into the book of Acts, a dramatic narrative shift has occurred. His followers now clearly mimic his actions, performing many of the same types of miracles he performed. They appear to be accessing the same power Jesus accessed, yielding the same results. Peter, Paul, Barnabas, Stephen, Philip, Ananias, and Agabus. All these men are named in the book of Acts as having performed miracles. The magic is spreading.

Chapter 16 of Acts tells of a girl possessed by a demon, "a spirit of divination."

Once when we [Paul and Silas] were going to the place of prayer, we were met by a female slave who ***had a spirit by which she predicted the future****. She earned a great deal of money for her owners by fortune-telling. She followed Paul and the rest of us, shouting, "These men are servants of the Most High God, who are telling you the way to be saved." She kept this up for many days. Finally Paul became so annoyed that he turned around and said to the spirit, "In the name of Jesus Christ I command you to come out of her!" At that moment the spirit left her.*

In this passage, the source of the girl's power is identified as a demonic spirit. Oddly though, the powers exhibited by this young girl are the very same precognitive powers as those of Daniel, one of the bible's great heroes.

Then, in Acts 13:

They [Paul and Barnabas] ... met a Jewish sorcerer and false prophet named Bar-Jesus, who was an attendant of the proconsul, Sergius Paulus. The proconsul, an intelligent man, sent for Barnabas and Saul because he wanted to hear the word of God. But Elymas ***the sorcerer*** *(for that is what his name means) opposed them and tried to turn the proconsul from the faith. Then Saul, who was also called Paul, filled with the Holy Spirit, looked straight at Elymas and said, "****You are a child of the devil*** *and an enemy of everything that is right! You are full of all kinds of deceit and trickery. Will you never stop perverting the right ways of the Lord? Now the* *hand of the Lord is against you.* ***You are going to be blind for a time****, not even able to see the light of the sun." Immediately mist and darkness came over him, and he groped about, seeking someone to lead him by the hand.*

Here, the apostle Paul accuses Elymas, aka "Bar-Jesus", of demonic influence, calling him a child of the devil. Paul then proceeds to place a spell of temporary blindness upon the man. Here we have clear evidence of magic being used by opposing men. This is not a case of God working through men. These men are not merely channeling divine power. They are intentional agents of power, able to enact supernatural results on their own accord, through magical means. They are wizards.

Healing Muses

Wizards are not the only magic-users in the pages of the bible. King David is a prominent figure in the books of first and second Samuel, and is portrayed as the quintessential bard. His music is said to have cast a calming spell upon his listeners. In medieval Gaelic and British culture, a bard was a professional storyteller, verse-maker, music composer, oral historian and genealogist, weaving magic through words and music to inspire allies, demoralize foes, manipulate minds, create illusions, and even heal wounds. The bible devotes a large chunk of its pages to this tradition in the Psalms and Proverbs of David and Solomon.

1 Samuel 16 tells how David's musical talents led him to the royal palace.

Now the Spirit of the Lord had departed from Saul, and an evil spirit from the Lord tormented him. Saul's attendants said to him, "See, an evil spirit from God is tormenting you. Let our lord command his servants here to search for someone who can play the lyre. He will play when the evil spirit from God comes on you, and you will feel better."

So Saul said to his attendants, "Find someone who plays well and bring him to me." One of the servants answered, "I have seen a son of Jesse of Bethlehem who knows how to play the lyre. He is a brave man and a warrior. He speaks well and is a fine-looking man. And the Lord is with him." Then Saul sent messengers to

Jesse and said, "Send me your son David, who is with the sheep." So Jesse took a donkey loaded with bread, a skin of wine and a young goat and sent them with his son David to Saul.

David came to Saul and entered his service. Saul liked him very much, and David became one of his armor-bearers. Then Saul sent word to Jesse, saying, "Allow David to remain in my service, for I am pleased with him." Whenever the spirit from God came on Saul, David would take up his lyre and play. Then relief would come to Saul; he would feel better, and the evil spirit would leave him.

Many of David's lyrics have been captured in the Psalms and continue to be a rich source of comfort to millions to this day. Perhaps his best known line, comes from Psalm 23:

Yea, though I walk through the valley of the shadow of death, I will fear no evil: for thou art with me

It speaks of a blessing of safety, almost like a protective spell. In fact, this phrase is often used in practice, as a sort of charm. It is repeated from memory, the very act of which causes a sense of calm within the mind of the reciter. This is the power of the ancient bardic magic.

The Bronze Serpent

In chapter 21 of the book of Numbers we read of yet another divine curse, and a strange antidote in the form of a magical item.

But the people grew impatient on the way; they spoke against God and against Moses, and said, "Why have you brought us up out of Egypt to die in the wilderness? There is no bread! There is no water! And we detest this miserable food!"

Then the Lord sent venomous snakes among them; they bit the people and many Israelites died. The people came to Moses and said, "We sinned when we spoke against the Lord and against you. Pray that the Lord will take the snakes away from us." So Moses prayed for the people.

The Lord said to Moses, "Make a snake and put it up on a pole; anyone who is bitten can look at it and live." So Moses made a bronze snake and put it up on a pole. Then when anyone was bitten by a snake and looked at the bronze snake, they lived.

This magic bronze serpent amulet somehow had power to counteract snake venom simply by eye contact.

The artifact was kept for at least five hundred years as a historical item until it was ordered destroyed by King Hezekiah as part of his iconoclastic reforms, documented in 2 Kings 18:4. Even thousands of years ago, divinely inspired magic items were cause for controversy.

The Ark Of The Covenant

The Ark of the Covenant is one of ancient Israel's most powerful magic items. It caused the Jordan River to dry up as soon as the feet of the priests carrying the Ark touched its waters.

At Jericho, the Ark was carried around the city seven times, accompanied by bardic magic in the form of seven horn trumpets. This ritual, culminating with a great shout, magically caused the collapse of the city wall.

Aside from the powerful benefits it provided, the Ark's powers were actually pretty hazardous. On several occasions it caused the accidental deaths of hapless or careless people who touched it. The Ark had to be handled with great care. Ceremonial methods were prescribed to ensure proper procedures for safety. The Ark was placed in a separate room in a sacred temple, and only the high priest could enter its presence.

For hundreds of years, the Ark remained the holiest artifact in Judaism, and was closely guarded and protected by top secret missions during times of warfare, political unrest, and captivity. It is thought to remain hidden in secrecy to this day, and many theories abound as to its current location.

Hebrews 9:4 tells us that the ark of the covenant was covered on all sides with gold, and contained several other magic artifacts, including a golden jar of manna,

Aaron's rod which had miraculously budded, and the stone tablets upon which were written the ten commandments.

It is said that the real power of the Ark came not from the physical artifacts it contained, but rather, from a spiritual presence upon it. The ark is thought to be the spatial location for the actual manifestation of the presence of God. Jehovah himself is thought to rest within a space upon the top of the Ark, between the wings of two golden angelic sculptures upon its lid. Thus, the Ark contains the divine presence.

The Divine Presence

The Divine Presence is the curse breaker. The blessing of divine presence overrides any and all curses.

Yet, somehow this presence is a two sided coin. The location of Jehovah between the wings of the cherubim atop the Ark is referred to as "the mercy seat". This can be more accurately translated from Hebrew as the seat of propitiation. Propitiation carries with it a dual implication. There is the concept of appeasement. This idea is only meaningful in relation to a deeper, underlying, yet unspoken meaning. That of the punisher. The vengeful angry god who must be feared. The one whose wrath must be appeased. This is the classic picture of the white-bearded old man doling out judgement. And it's a picture that's not entirely inaccurate.

It was God who set in place the curse of Adam. It was God who set in place the rules that Moses and his crew could never seem to keep, and the curses that come along with breaking these rules. God's presence upon the Ark of the covenant was a deadly powerful force. It was not to be taken lightly. God is the embodiment of the curse, just as he is of the blessing. He is the blessing and the curse. And we are made in his image.

Human Presence

In Psalms 82:6, God says to human beings: “You are gods, and all of you are children of the Most High.” The Hebrew word translated “gods” is Elohim, which literally means “gods” or “mighty ones”—although it is often rendered as “God” in the Bible. Yes, we are Elohim. We are the people of god, the divine people. Jesus himself quoted this passage in John 10

We are made in the image of God. Jesus juxtaposed himself as the son of man and the son of God. He exemplified our human and divine presence. He showed that to be, is to be god. our presence is God’s presence. We are gods.

We are both the blessing and the curse. We are both the curse and the blessing. It is our agency, our free will, our sentience that provides any meaning. Our divine existence is the purpose. We are magic.

Name Dropping

The book of Acts is rife with stories of magical actions performed by ordinary men. How did they do it? They recognized the divine magic within them, as shown to them by their teacher, Jesus. They walked in his ways. They worked in his methods. They identified in his name. Jesus said in Mark 16:

And these signs shall follow them that believe; In my name shall they cast out devils; they shall speak with new tongues; they shall take up serpents; and if they drink any deadly thing, it shall not hurt them; they shall lay hands on the sick, and they shall recover.

Here, Jesus prophesies that his followers will act in his name and perform magical feats. Many examples too numerous to list can be found of Jesus' prophecy playing out. "In the name of Jesus" becomes a very common phrase throughout the rest of the new testament. And its use is accompanied by all manner of wondrous miracles. The name of Jesus seems to be used as a magical incantation. The mention of his name causes powers to shift.

The following story from Acts 19 is a particularly telling example, as it provides a bit of a peek behind the curtains.

God did extraordinary miracles through Paul, so that even handkerchiefs and aprons that had touched him were taken to the sick, and their illnesses were cured and the evil spirits left them.

Some Jews who went around driving out evil spirits tried to invoke the name of the Lord Jesus over those who were demon-possessed. They would say, "In the name of the Jesus whom Paul preaches, I command you to come out." Seven sons of Sceva, a Jewish chief priest, were doing this. One day the evil spirit answered them, "Jesus I know, and Paul I know about, but who are you?" Then the man who had the evil spirit jumped on them and overpowered them all. He gave them such a beating that they ran out of the house naked and bleeding.

When this became known to the Jews and Greeks living in Ephesus, they were all seized with fear, and the name of the Lord Jesus was held in high honor.

These healers knew a good thing when they saw it. They witnessed the successful healings performed by Paul and they sought to incorporate his methods into their practice, taking on the terminology used by Paul. But since these men did not know Jesus personally, they attached a parenthetical phrase—*In the name of Jesus whom Paul preaches*.

It didn't work. The name and the power were a step removed. They failed to integrate their identity with that of Jesus. They didn't recognize the divinity of their humanity. They were strangers to and in the magical realm. They had no connection of their own.

Jesus speaks of this disconnection in Matthew 7:

Not everyone who says to me, 'Lord, Lord,' will enter the kingdom of heaven, but the one who does the will of my Father who is in heaven. On that day many will say to me, 'Lord, Lord, did we not prophesy in your name, and cast out demons in your name, and do many mighty works in your name?' And then I will say to them, 'I never knew you: depart from me, ye that work iniquity'.

Jesus exposes the false notion that rational logic is the ultimate answer in life. Life is complex and weird. It is filled with both blessings and curses. It may appear that a simple and straight-forward method exists, by which we might be saved. Jesus says this is not the case. He twists the logic back upon itself.

Jesus is quoting the bard, David from Psalm 6: *Depart from me, all ye workers of iniquity; for the Lord hath heard the voice of my weeping.*

The psalm bears repeating in its entirety for it is both brief and complex. It weaves together the blessing and the curse that is God and the blessing and curse that it is to be human. It is desperation and grief and faith and supplication and torment and revenge.

- Psalm 6 -

O Lord, rebuke me not in thine anger, neither chasten me in thy hot displeasure.

Have mercy upon me, O Lord; for I am weak: O Lord, heal me; for my bones are vexed.

My soul is also sore vexed: but thou, O Lord, how long?

Return, O Lord, deliver my soul: oh save me for thy mercies' sake.

For in death there is no remembrance of thee: in the grave who shall give thee thanks?

I am weary with my groaning; all the night make I my bed to swim; I water my couch with my tears.

Mine eye is consumed because of grief; it waxeth old because of all mine enemies.

Depart from me, all ye workers of iniquity; for the Lord hath heard the voice of my weeping.

The Lord hath heard my supplication; the Lord will receive my prayer.

Let all mine enemies be ashamed and sore vexed: let them return and be ashamed suddenly.

Conclusion

The human condition is a mass of contradictions. Like David, we both blame God and cry out to him in the same breath. We call curses upon our enemies. We seek blessings. We yearn for personal power. For identity, for fairness, justice, and peace. We long to connect intimately with a higher power that we can never hope to truly understand. We feel, in this urge, such import, such urgency, that we can only say we are created for just such a connection. We feel within our very lives a sense of magic, and we fear to wield its power well.

Nothing is simple. Nothing is what it seems. Perhaps it is a sobering realization to know that our tendency to oversimplify may have led us into false assumptions. Perhaps everything is more complicated than we like to think and we need assistance to navigate our way out of dualistic thinking. Perhaps this is the true magic of the bible. Jesus himself shows this paradox. Sometimes he chooses a simplistic representation. He boils all of the law, and morality, and ethics down into a single word. "Love." He says. At other times, Jesus presents an impossible goal; "I only do what the father is doing." Perhaps the greatest magic comes in integrating these two paradoxical statements.

Thank You

Thank you for reading this book. I hope you found both interesting and thought-provoking. Please consider leaving a review on Goodreads.com or Amazon.

If you would like to see my other books, check out my author page at https://dimensionfold.com/authors/ken-goudsward/

and join my mailing list at https://dimensionfold.com/join/

Made in United States
Orlando, FL
09 December 2024

55257682R00055